P. J. G. Ransom

Transport in Scotl [CW00919189]
Through the Ages

Illustrated by John Marshall

Richard Drew Publishing, Glasgow

Note: you will probably find it helpful to have a map of Scotland handy while reading this book, and you will also find further information about Scottish transport in other Otter Books — *Great Scottish Discoveries and Inventions* and *Great Scottish Feats of Engineering and Building*.

British Library Cataloguing in Publication Data
Ransom, P. J. G.
Transport in Scotland through the ages. — (Otter)
1. Transportation — Scotland — History — Juvenile literature
I. Title   II. Series
380.5'09411   HE245
ISBN 0-86267-182-5
ISBN 0-86267-181-7 Pbk

First Published 1987 by Richard Drew Ltd.
6 Clairmont Gardens, Glasgow G3 7LW

Copyright © 1987 P J G Ransom

Designed by James W Murray
Printed and bound in Great Britain
Set in Raleigh by John Swain Ltd, Glasgow

What This Book is About

Most of us, when we travel, do so by car or bus. Or do we? We also travel by bicycle or train, motor coach or aeroplane, ship, boat or ferry. The list goes on and on. But how are there so many types of transport? And why do we choose one rather than another?

Well, one reason is that Scotland is such a varied country: Highlands and Lowlands, open country and big cities, sea lochs and firths, and a great many off-shore islands. Different parts of the country require different forms of transport, and we choose the most suitable. Another reason is that we travel by the means we – or our parents – can afford.

There is another, very important, reason. Think of it like this: perhaps you live in a village beneath a railway viaduct which no longer carries trains. Or perhaps a canal runs along the hillside behind your town, but no barges go along it. There is much to be seen of means of transport that people used to use but do not any more. Why did they stop using them?

The quick answer is that when new forms of transport were invented, people found them quicker or cheaper or more convenient than old ones – so when steam trains were invented they stopped using horse-drawn coaches, when buses and cars came along they stopped using trains. But like all quick answers it is not a complete one. Something else is remarkable about transport in Scotland: old means of transport often survive alongside newer ones. Horse-drawn milk floats have only just ceased delivering in Edinburgh, and jet aircraft roar over parts of the Highlands where roads have never been made and there are only footpaths. There are still places on the West Coast such as Inverie, in Knoydart, to which there are no roads – they are reached by walking, or by boat.

So, how did all this come about? It is not a simple story, but, more or less, it happened this way . . .

The First Travellers
From the earliest times to 1500

To walk, or (if wealthy enough) ride a horse or pony, or go by boat, rowed or sailed: these were the choices open to most of our ancestors who wished to travel. This was so in prehistoric times, and it remained so until as recently as about 300 years ago. Originally, much of Scotland, as well as being mountainous, was covered by forest, so the easiest way to travel long distances was by boat along the coast. Prehistoric men knew enough about boats to reach Orkney and Lewis and set up immense circles of standing stones. The Roman fleet reached Scotland. Viking ships were so dependable that the Vikings from Scandinavia not only raided but settled on the Scottish coast and islands. In the fifteenth century, King James IV had a great navy built of wooden sailing ships.

On land, in prehistoric times the easiest routes between settlements no doubt became trampled into paths by the feet of passing travellers and their animals. Roads, with good foundations and gravel surfaces, were first made by the Romans. Their most important road originated at Corbridge on Hadrian's Wall, crossed the Cheviot Hills and then continued towards Edinburgh. Roman roads in Scotland extended to a total length of about 450 miles, and on them wheeled vehicles made their first appearance, for the Romans had both wagons and chariots.

People went on using the Roman roads during the dark and middle ages, though wagons and carts were almost unknown; goods were carried on packhorses. Travel was difficult and dangerous. Wolves inhabited the forests. There were few bridges – rivers had to be crossed by fords or ferries. All people were affected, poor or rich. When King Alexander III attempted a night journey on horseback, in 1286, his horse slipped and he was thrown and killed. The result was three centuries of warfare, on and off, between Scotland and England, for with no strong king in Scotland, King Edward I of England decided to invade.

This is the type of ship used by the Vikings between Orkney and Norway.

As recently as 200 years ago, there was no road system for wheeled vehicles north of Inverness, and even famous travellers such as Dr Johnson had to ride or walk.

Early Roads and Their Users
1300 – 1760

Some of the earliest roads were 'drove roads'. These were traditional routes, not roads with hard surfaces such as we have today. Throughout the Highlands, cattle were driven south along them for sale at Crieff or Falkirk. Cattle droving started late in the middle ages and increased gradually over the centuries: large herds of cattle on the move became the first really busy road traffic in Scotland.

In 1603 a postal service was set up on the road from Edinburgh to Berwick. At several places on the route, the king appointed postmasters to provide horses for riders carrying letters, both for the government and for other people too. Each postmaster provided a horse to carry the rider as far as the next place which had a postmaster. The same system was already in use in England between Berwick and London, and on other roads there.

From this start the Scottish postal service was gradually extended to link Edinburgh with Glasgow, Portpatrick (for the sea crossing to Ireland) and elsewhere. Some services were 'riding posts' but many were 'foot posts' – the letters were carried, sometimes over very long distances, by men who walked.

To try to improve the roads, the Scottish Parliament in 1669 passed an Act to set up, by law, a system called 'statute labour'. This meant that every summer all the tenants and servants in each parish had to spend six days or so repairing its roads and bridges. They did not know much about roadwork, but they knew as much as anybody else. In charge were the government officials for each county, and landowners were taxed to pay for the work. Later on, most people were allowed to make a payment towards the cost of keeping the roads in repair, instead of working on them personally.

Statute labour did result in gradual improvements of roads in the Lowlands, but had little effect in the Highlands – just because it was so difficult for officials to travel there that the government could not make people obey the laws. Then in 1707 came the Act of Union which joined Scotland and England together in the United Kingdom, and in 1715 after the death of Queen Anne the Jacobites made an armed rising. They supported the claim of James Edward

Cattle droving: cattle are loaded on board the ferry at Kyleakin, Skye, for transport to the mainland.

A riding post.

Stewart, a catholic, to be king instead of protestant King George I. Most Jacobite support came from the Highlands, and after the rising had been put down General Wade suggested that a network of roads should be built there for troops to move around easily. These 'military roads' were built mainly by soldiers. They had foundations of boulders and surfaces of gravel, and many bridges to carry them over burns and rivers. Wade's first road went from Fort William to Fort Augustus and Inverness. Next he built two roads which ran northwards from Dunkeld and Crieff, joined into one through the pass of Drumochter and then split apart to go to Fort Augustus and Inverness. Eventually over 1000 miles of military roads were built.

These roads were used by everyone, not just soldiers, and although their hills were steep they were usually passable for carts and carriages. Wheeled vehicles were slowly being used more and more. In some districts people used slide cars, or wheel-less carts. These looked like a pair of shafts extending so far behind the horse that their ends could slide along the ground; a platform built upon them carried the load. When someone added a pair of wheels beneath the platform, the result was a wheeled cart.

The First Coaches

Archbishop Sharp is murdered, 1679.

King Alexander III had been travelling on horseback when he was killed, but when Archbishop Sharp was murdered by Covenanters in 1679 they pulled him from his coach. Important people were gradually starting to use coaches. These were drawn by four or six horses and were lumbering great vehicles without springs – to us they would seem terribly slow and uncomfortable. In 1740 Lord Lovat set out in his coach with his daughters to travel from Beauly, Inverness-shire, to London. But the military roads were rough, and the coach was damaged so badly and so often that it took him twelve days to get as far as Edinburgh. In that city itself, with its wynds and closes, people preferred sedan chairs to coaches.

However in and around Edinburgh there was so much traffic – packhorses, slide cars, carts, coaches – that in 1713 gates had been placed across the roads at which all traffic had to stop to pay tolls. The money raised was used for improving and maintaining the roads. The gates were called turnpikes, and this was the first instance in Scotland of their use. Later in the century wheeled traffic increased and people working under statute labour were unable to look after their roads properly. So most main roads in the Lowlands were made into 'turnpike roads'. Parliament set up 'turnpike trusts', which were groups of landowners and other wealthy people, to run the turnpike roads, and travellers became used to finding, every fifteen miles or so, a turnpike gate with the gatekeeper's house beside it at which they must stop to pay a toll.

The first coaches were private ones, and early attempts to run coach services for the public did not last long because too few people wished to travel. However by the 1740s there was a regular coach service between Edinburgh and Leith, and in the 1750s successful coach services started between Edinburgh and Glasgow, and Edinburgh and London. Then, as the roads improved, public coach services gradually spread throughout the Lowlands. 'Stage coaches', they were called, because the horses were changed at the end of each stage of about ten miles. This was often done at inns run by the postmasters. Postmasters also provided relays of horses for carriages called post chaises which wealthy travellers could hire.

and Turnpike Roads
1650 – 1800

The mail coach of 1786.

The earliest stage coaches were slow (the Edinburgh-Glasgow coach at first took two days, with an overnight stop at Falkirk) and unreliable – their proprietors were often unwilling to say which day they would arrive, let alone what time. But in 1784, between Bristol and London, John Palmer introduced the first mail coach: a coach which travelled fast through the night, with a guard armed against highwaymen, and so carried the letters far more quickly and safely than a riding post. It also carried a limited number of passengers. It was an instant success, and the Post Office then started mail coach services between London and other important cities, including Edinburgh in 1786 and Glasgow two years later. Mail coaches had springs, and ran to timetables which said when they would arrive, to the nearest minute. Everything else on the road had to give way to the mail.

Of course this meant that owners of stage coaches had to make them faster and more comfortable too, or they would have lost their passengers.

Canals are Built
1759 — 1815

The Firth of Clyde and the Firth of Forth are only about thirty five miles apart, and as early as the seventeenth century people started to think of digging a canal - that is, a man-made waterway - between them. Along it, ships would be able to go across Scotland from one coast to the other.

Then between 1759 and 1765 the Duke of Bridgewater had a canal built to carry coal from his mines at Worsley into Manchester, seven and a half miles away. This was the first cross-country canal in Britain and was so successful that it started a wave of enthusiasm for canal building. John Smeaton, greatest British engineer of the day, produced plans for a canal between Forth and Clyde. Another route was surveyed by James Watt, who later became famous for his improvements to the steam engines already then used to pump water out of coal mines. But for the canal Smeaton's route was preferred and in 1768 Parliament passed an Act which set up a company to build and run the Forth & Clyde Canal. People bought shares in the company to pay for building the canal and eventually, they hoped, enough money would come in from payments by people using the canal for the shareholders in turn to receive

Kelvin Aqueduct.

payments called dividends. This was how the money was raised to pay for building most canals, and later for railways.

The Forth and Clyde Canal was 2·13m (7ft) deep, and it had forty locks which enabled small ships to climb up and over high ground. It was opened from the Forth, where the port of Grangemouth later grew up around the entrance lock, through Falkirk to Kirkintilloch by 1773, to Glasgow (on a short branch from the main line) in 1777, and to the Clyde at Bowling in 1790. An aqueduct 21·35m (70ft) high carried the canal over the River Kelvin.

The canal was a great success. Along it horses pulled boats, barges and small ships: these carried coal, timber, grain and iron, and all manner of merchandise. They also carried passengers. The 'passage boats' were a smooth and comfortable alternative to road coaches.

Other canals were soon built elsewhere in Scotland. Among them, the Monkland Canal (engineered by James Watt) brought coal into Glasgow from the area around Coatbridge, and the Crinan Canal provided a short cut for small ships across the Mull of Kintyre. The Caledonian Canal was built through the Great Glen: lengths of wide and deep canal linked Loch Ness and other lochs with east and west coasts, so that ships could avoid the stormy passage round the north of Scotland. The engineer who planned it and supervised its construction was Thomas Telford, the son of a Borders shepherd, who had trained as a stone mason and risen to become a famous engineer.

About 1806 Telford planned a canal between Glasgow and Ardrossan where, it was intended, ships would transfer cargoes into canal barges bound for Glasgow. In those days the Clyde was not deep enough for large ships to reach Glasgow itself, and they unloaded their cargoes into barges down river. But within a few years the Clyde itself was made deeper so the canal was never completed, although the section which was built from Glasgow to Paisley and Johnstone was busy for many years. Once ships could reach Glasgow by the Clyde, more and more quays were built along its banks. As well as building canals at this period people were busy improving ports. Docks were built at Leith and Dundee, and Aberdeen harbour was much improved by Telford.

A sailing ship is towed along Loch Oich while passing through the Caledonian Canal.

Before railways were built, canals provided the transport for Glasgow industries.

Horse Railways and Highland Roads
1722 – 1815

Telford inspects progress on the Highland Roads, 1819.

Throughout this period when roads were improved and canals were built, the problem of bad transport was being solved in a different way by owners of coal mines. They laid wagonways – which were like later railways, but with rails of wood – between mines and harbours, and along them horses pulled wagons of coal for shipment. The first wagonway in Scotland had been built in 1722 between Tranent and Cockenzie harbour on the Forth. Along its low embankment, during the Jacobite rising of 1745, General Sir John Cope positioned government troops and cannon – only to be routed by Bonnie Prince Charlie's forces when they attacked out of the early morning mists. This, the battle of Prestonpans, was the only time a railway in Britain has been fought over.

About 1800, rails made of cast iron became available. They wore out much less quickly than wooden ones, and so gradually replaced them. Temporary railways with iron rails were used to move earth and rock during construction of the Caledonian Canal. The Kilmarnock & Troon Railway, opened in 1811, was the first public railway in Scotland: a company, like a canal company, had been formed to build it, and, like a turnpike road, anyone could pay a toll to take a horse-drawn wagon on it (provided it fitted the track).

Meanwhile, transport in the Highlands was being greatly improved. By about 1800, risings and battles were things of the past and the military roads were no longer needed for their original purpose. But about 600 miles were still maintained for public use, although needing improvement, and roads and bridges were needed in districts where they were still lacking. This was one of

Telford's bridge over the River Spey at Craigellachie.

the recommendations made by Telford when the Government sent him to survey and report on the Highlands in 1802. Making the Caledonian Canal was another, and so was improvement of many harbours, mainly for fishing boats.

Although cattle droving was now at its height, and every autumn immense herds could be seen moving slowly southwards, some landowners were replacing cattle farming by sheep. These needed fewer people to tend them, and as a result Highlanders were losing their work, and their homes; they started to emigrate. Telford hoped to provide jobs and reduce emigration.

In 1803 Parliament set up 'the Commissioners for making Roads and building Bridges in the Highlands of Scotland', and agreed to contribute half the cost of the new roads and bridges if the landowners contributed the other half. With Telford as their engineer, the commissioners then built 920 miles of roads and a great many bridges, large and small, over the next eighteen years. Telford's roads were better than the military roads - they were wider, with easy slopes and gentle curves for trotting horses. Their surface was of gravel so cattle, when driven long distances over them, had their hoofs shod with iron shoes like horseshoes. Most of the new roads were in the Northern Highlands; the most important new bridges were at Dunkeld, Craigellachie and Bonar Bridge. Many of the surviving military roads were transferred to the commissioners to maintain, although the important sections in Perthshire were turnpiked. With all these improvements, wheeled vehicles could at last travel to the far North of Scotland: in 1819 a mail coach started to run to Thurso, replacing a foot post.

Struy Bridge, Inverness-shire, is typical of those built for the Highland Roads, and is still in use.

Bridge over the River Irvine, Ayrshire, was built about 1812 for the horse-drawn trains of the Kilmarnock & Troon Railway.

Steam in the Era

A Clyde steam boat of about 1816.

Paddle steamer *James Watt*, built by Wood & Co. who had built Bell's *Comet*, entered service between Leith and London in 1821.

The first steam engines were stationary ones, gigantic steam pumps (two or three storeys high) used from 1712 onwards to drain mines. James Watt made them work efficiently with his invention of the 'separate condenser' in 1765 and by the 1780s steam engines were being built which would work machinery. In them, a fire beneath a boiler produced steam: the pressure of this was used to push a piston to and fro in a cylinder, and the piston was connected by rods and a crank to a shaft, making it turn to drive the machinery.

Many people were attracted by the idea of making compact steam engines and using them to drive boats or carriages. By 1783 Frenchmen had made both a steam carriage and a steam boat that would work, though they were not reliable enough to be used regularly. In 1800 William Symington of Leadhills, Lanarkshire, who had made earlier experiments, was invited to build the engine for a steam tug boat for the Forth & Clyde Canal. After three years of trials he had produced an engine of simple and efficient design which was fitted in the specially built boat *Charlotte Dundas*. This, the first successful steam boat, showed her strength in March 1803 when she towed two other vessels for nineteen and a half miles into a gale so strong that horses could not move boats to windward at all. But because it was feared her wash would damage the canal banks she did not go into regular service.

Two people who knew of Symington's work were American Robert Fulton, who obtained an engine from the British firm of Boulton, Watt & Co., took it to New York and installed it in the *Clermont* with which he started the world's first successful steamer service in 1807, and Henry Bell, who with his little paddle steamer *Comet* started the first steamer service in Europe in 1812, down the Clyde from Glasgow to Greenock.

Now, a sailing boat could travel only where and when the wind and tide would take her, but a reliable steam boat was mostly independent of these. Once *Comet* had shown this, other steam boats were quickly built, and six years later there were about eighteen at work carrying passengers and goods on the Clyde. Others were working on the Forth, the Tay and Loch Lomond. Within a few years paddle steamers were being used extensively

# of Horsedrawn Transport
1780 – 1840

on coastal routes and were bringing the advantages of mechanical transport to remote Scottish islands at a time when travel throughout most of Britain still meant horse-drawn carriages.

Attempts to build steam carriages were much less successful than those to build steam boats – roads were still not good enough for heavy, clumsy vehicles – and the first attempts to build steam railway locomotives were not much better. From 1814 onwards George Stephenson, who was in charge of the steam pumps at Killingworth colliery near Newcastle upon Tyne, built a series of steam locomotives, each slightly better than the last, for the colliery wagonway; the first he built to work elsewhere was supplied in 1817 to the Kilmarnock & Troon Railway. But it did not work well enough for regular use. One problem was that rails were still of cast iron, which is brittle, and too many were broken under the weight of the locomotives. By 1818 rails of malleable iron, which is less brittle, had been invented and these were used on the second public railway in Scotland, the Monkland & Kirkintilloch opened in 1826, although at first horses pulled its trains.

Despite the invention of steamships, sailing ships continued to be used for many years. These are Forth ferries in Leith Harbour, 1822.

A coal train pulled by a horse: Monkland & Kirkintilloch Railway.

'Swift' boats carried passengers on the Forth & Clyde Canal in the 1830s.

The London-Glasgow mail coach.

Then in 1829 the directors of the Liverpool & Manchester Railway, whose line was nearly complete, held a competition called the Rainhill Trials to find a locomotive which would be a decided improvement on any made so far. This was won by *Rocket*, entered by a partnership of George Stephenson, his son Robert and Henry Booth who had suggested an improved design of boiler. So *Rocket* was both powerful and, by the standards of the time, fast – able to run at 30 mph when horse-drawn coaches went at nine or ten. The advantages of such machines were obvious, and the Garnkirk & Glasgow Railway, opened in 1831, was equipped with locomotives of the latest Stephenson design.

Nevertheless such machines were too revolutionary for people to take full advantage of them straight away. The railways in Scotland were all still short ones, often used horses (even to pull passenger coaches) and were second in importance to water transport. The Monkland & Kirkintilloch brought coal down to the Forth & Clyde Canal, the Dundee & Newtyle (opened in 1831) linked fertile Strathmore with Dundee harbour. Rather, the 1820s and 1830s were the great era of canals, coaches and coastal steamers. Steamers carried cattle which would otherwise have been driven, and they carried the mails down the Clyde and to islands such as Islay. The Crinan and Caledonian Canals became part of the steamer route between Glasgow, Crinan, Fort William and Inverness.

The Edinburgh & Glasgow Union Canal, opened in 1822, completed the canal link between those two cities: in fact the Union

Canal, as it is called, left the Forth & Clyde near Falkirk, climbed through eleven locks close together and then continued on the same level all the way to Edinburgh, over 30 miles away. Like this, passing through locks caused least delay to boats; to achieve it the canal had to pass through a tunnel nearly 640m (700yds) long near Falkirk, and cross over three river valleys by high aqueducts. Passenger boats went between Glasgow and Edinburgh by day and by night, and following experiments on the Paisley Canal it was found that lightweight 'Swift Boats' pulled by two galloping horses could go at 10 mph.

Roads too were being improved. John McAdam had discovered that a smooth firm surface could be made from a layer of stones each about 5cm (2ins) across, given the grinding action of iron-tyred vehicles constantly passing over it. Many turnpike roads were rebuilt in this way. There was no tar in McAdam's roads – that was still to come. Telford rebuilt the Glasgow-Carlisle road using a surface like McAdam's on a strong foundation of carefully chosen large stones.

By the 1830s there were 24 mail coach services daily in Scotland, and 316 stage coaches. The *Erin-go-Bragh* coach ran through from Edinburgh to Dublin, being carried by ship between Portpatrick and Donaghadee in Ireland, but the most famous stage coach in Scotland, and the fastest, was the *Defiance* which covered the 129 miles from Edinburgh to Aberdeen via Perth in a little over 12 hours, including the ferry across the Forth. Not very fast by today's standards, but marvellous for a vehicle drawn by horses, and much faster than people were used to.

This was once a coaching inn and horse-changing point on the Glasgow-Carlisle road. Now it is Hamilton Museum.

Present-day travellers crossing Pathhead Bridge, on the A68 south of Edinburgh, probably do not realise it was designed by Telford so that coach horses could avoid steep hills.

Railways — The First Main Lines
1831 — 1901

One of the first locomotives of the Caledonian Railway.

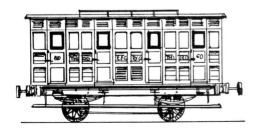

Third class coach, Edinburgh & Glasgow Railway.

The Garnick & Glasgow Railway ran parallel to the Monkland Canal: it too was intended to carry coal into Glasgow. It was the first Scottish railway to compete with water transport. On the opposite side of Glasgow, and in competition with the Paisley Canal, the Glasgow, Paisley, Kilmarnock & Ayr Railway was completed by 1840. But these were intended only as local lines. What Stephenson's locomotives had demonstrated on the Liverpool & Manchester Railway was that a steam railway could provide a link between two big cities which would be both quicker and cheaper than stage coaches, and carry more passengers too. Such main line railways were soon being built between London and Birmingham, and from Birmingham northwards to join the Liverpool & Manchester.

The first main line in Scotland was the Edinburgh & Glasgow Railway, opened in 1842 between Edinburgh (Haymarket) and Glasgow (Queen Street). A journey of five hours by coach was reduced to two hours by train. Within a couple of years there was immense enthusiasm throughout Scotland - indeed throughout the whole of Great Britain - for forming companies to build railways here, there and everywhere. It was called the Railway Mania. 'The country is become an asylum of railway lunatics,' commented Lord Cockburn, a noted Scottish judge, in 1845. Nevertheless in that year Parliament authorised construction of 423 miles of railways in Scotland including those which became the backbone of the Scottish Railway system.

By 1848 the Caledonian Railway was complete from Carlisle (reached by English railways from the South the same year) to Edinburgh and Glasgow, and other companies took the route onward to Stirling, Perth and (later) Aberdeen. The North British Railway was open from Edinburgh to Berwick, and other railways soon linked the capital with Perth and Dundee, although the Firths of Forth and Tay were still crossed by ferries. By the end of the 1850s the Lowlands were well-served by rail. It took much longer for railways to be built in the Highlands: in mountainous country they were expensive to build, and there was little traffic. Railways

did not reach Inverness until 1861, Wick and Thurso until 1874, Oban until 1880 and Mallaig until 1901.

Before the opening of the Edinburgh & Glasgow Railway, there were thirteen stage coaches between those two cities; three weeks afterwards, twelve of them had been withdrawn. Wherever railways were opened, the effect on coaching was equally devastating. Passengers, mails, parcels, all went by train instead. Coaching, except for short distances, collapsed in the Lowlands; in the Highlands, however, in areas which did not have railways, coaches continued to run and indeed new routes were opened up. The canals in central Scotland found their traffic declining, though the passenger boats between Edinburgh and Glasgow lasted longer than the stage coaches and were not withdrawn until six years after the railway was opened. From the 1860s onwards little steamships called 'puffers' were built: small enough to pass through the Forth & Clyde Canal, they carried goods between Glasgow, East and West Coast ports, and the islands. Cattle droving died out as cattle were sent by train instead.

Ballochmyle Viaduct, Ayrshire, carried the Glasgow & South Western Railway's line from Glasgow to Dumfries and Carlisle over 50 metres (170 feet) above the Water of Ayr.

The Inverness & Aberdeen Junction Railway crosses the River Spey, about 1860.

Travel and the Tourist
1880 – 1914

North British Railway express.

By the end of Queen Victoria's reign, main line railways linked cities, branch lines reached country towns, and suburban lines carried people to work in cities from their homes nearby. Most of the railways in Scotland, following amalgamations, were run by five companies, which had also taken over the canals of central Scotland. The Paisley canal had even been filled in and its course used for a railway.

The Government encouraged railway companies to compete against each other – this kept the fares low. The London & North Western Railway ran trains from London (Euston) to Carlisle, and the Caledonian Railway took them on to Glasgow, Edinburgh and the North. This was the 'West Coast Route'. The Midland Railway also ran trains to Carlisle, from London St Pancras: the Glasgow & South Western Railway took these forward to Glasgow via Dumfries, and the North British Railway to Edinburgh via Hawick. The NBR also took trains of the 'East Coast Route' (from London King's Cross) – from Berwick to Edinburgh and beyond.

Every August wealthy and fashionable people travelled to the Highlands for the grouse shooting. Around 7.30 am trains from all three routes converged on Perth and, while their passengers breakfasted on Tay salmon in the refreshment room, vehicles going through were shunted to make one immensely long train for the Highland Railway to take to Inverness. On 7 August 1888, for instance, this comprised no less than 36 vehicles from 9 different companies: it needed two engines in front, and another behind to bank it from Blair Atholl to the 452·44m (1484ft) summit at Druimuachdar, the highest on a British main line.

Highland Railway train, double-headed.

Caledonian Railway No. 123 hauled West Coast expresses during the 'races to the North' of 1888, and can now be seen in Glasgow Museum of Transport.

In 1888 came the first railway 'races' to the North. The West Coast companies suddenly accelerated their overnight train from London to Edinburgh; the East Coast responded by accelerating theirs, until each route was alternately running specials as fast as it could, and the time came down from ten hours to eight. Once the Forth Bridge was opened (in 1890) the East Coast Route had, with the Tay Bridge opened earlier, the shortest route from London to Aberdeen: in 1895 racing broke out again. The public was enthusiastic: when, on

23 August 1895, the West Coast special ran the 540 miles from London to Aberdeen in 512 minutes, the crowd carried the driver and fireman shoulder high from the engine.

In the western Highlands tourists found a unique system of connecting trains, steamers and horse-drawn coaches. Consider the choices facing a tourist wishing to view the scenery between Glasgow and Oban about 1900. He could go by through train via Stirling and Callander. He could go (the shortest route) by train to Balloch, up Loch Lomond by steamer, and then by coach to rejoin a train at Crianlarich. He could take a big steamer – probably MacBrayne's famous paddle steamer *Columba* – down the Clyde to Ardrishaig, a small steamer through the Crinan Canal and a bigger one on to Oban, or take a coach from Ardrishaig to Loch Awe, a steamer up the loch and a train onwards, or go by steamer all the way round the Mull of Kintyre. Or he could take a train by the new West Highland line as far as Crianlarich and change for Oban. And when he did arrive, there were 30 or 40 steamers, trains and coaches leaving Oban daily to tempt him further.

Paddle steamers leave the Broomielaw, Glasgow, for destinations down the Clyde.

Clyde paddle steamers competed for passengers, and 'raced' to get them to their destinations first.

Trams, Bicycles and Motor Cars
1840 – 1914

Horse-drawn trams in Edinburgh.

Electric trams and early motor cars in Glasgow.

Passenger transport in cities, from the 1840s onwards , was often provided by horse-drawn omnibuses. Horse-drawn trams, which carried more people because they ran more freely on rails set into the road surface, first ran in Scotland in Edinburgh in 1871 and were soon introduced elsewhere. The first electric trams in Scotland, drawing current from overhead wires and driven by electric motors, ran in Glasgow in 1898. They were an efficient means of moving large quantities of people, and within a few years there were electric tramways in most large towns and cities in Scotland.

A passenger alighting from a train at a country railway station during the last century found that local transport was still almost entirely horse-drawn – carriages and carts. But, as railways spread, roads became less important. The Commissioners for the Highland Roads and Bridges were abolished in 1862; in the 1880s turnpikes, statute labour and road tolls were all abolished as well, and when county councils were first formed in 1889, they took over the roads and maintained them. The cost of doing so was met from taxes called rates.

And on these quiet roads there appeared the first hint of the coming revival of road traffic: the bicycle. Scotsman Kirkpatrick Macmillan made the first bicycle driven by pedals in 1839, but it was not until the 1870s that the idea started to catch on. Bicycles of this period had solid tyres and were very bumpy to ride. In 1888 J B Dunlop devised a pneumatic tyre – a circular tube of rubber inflated with air: these smoothed out the bumps and bicycling suddenly became very popular.

From about 1850 steam traction engines had been built to haul heavy loads by road. The first motor cars were developed abroad, mostly in Germany in the 1880s. Because they used internal combustion engines – fuel such as petrol is burned internally, within the cylinders, rather than externally in a separate boiler – they were lighter, more compact and more efficient than steam vehicles. But it was many years before they became as reliable.

In Scotland, the first motor car arrived at Leith on a steamship in October 1895. It was soon followed by others. About 1902 someone

The 1908 Argyll motor car.

Albion butcher's van, 1910.

put a van body on to one of them for the first time and used it to deliver goods. The bicycle and the lightweight petrol engine were combined to produce the motor cycle. Meanwhile, in 1899 the first motor bus service in Scotland had started, in Edinburgh between the Post Office and Haymarket. In 1904 the Great North of Scotland Railway started a motor bus service between Ballater and Braemar, and other bus services were soon established so that by 1910 there were about 600 motor buses in Scotland.

Pneumatic tyres were soon fitted to early motor vehicles, but they had one great disadvantage. They sucked dust out of the road surfaces so that rainwater penetrated and damaged them. Puddles became deep potholes. The solution was to coat roads with waterproof tar which also kept the gravel in place. This was the origin of tarred roads.

Invention of the internal combustion engine had another very important consequence: it was light enough to power a flying machine and make men's centuries-old dream of flying come true. Bicycle-makers Wilbur and Orville Wright were the first to fly an aeroplane successfully, in the USA in 1903. In 1909 Frank and Harold Barnwell flew an aeroplane they had built near Stirling: the first aeroplane to fly in Scotland.

Edinburgh-Corstorphine motor bus, about 1906.

Road versus Rail
1914 – 1945

During the First World War all forms of transport were extremely busy moving troops and war supplies. Motor vehicles and aircraft benefited because they were built in large quantities to new and improved designs; railways suffered because heavy traffic wore them out while the men who would have maintained them were away fighting. In 1922 railways throughout Britain were grouped into four large companies: the North British and Great North of Scotland Railways became part of the London & North Eastern Railway, and the Caledonian, Glasgow & South Western and Highland Railways became part of the London Midland & Scottish.

Passengers, however, were finding that motor buses which called in the centres of villages were more convenient than trains which called at stations some way off. Motor lorries were carrying more and more goods direct from factory to factory or farm to market. From the late 1920s onwards, railways started to close branch lines and country stations which had lost too much traffic to road transport. Towns with electric trams were replacing them by cheaper buses, long-distance motor coach routes were introduced (such as London to Glasgow, 403 miles which, in vehicles limited to 30 mph, took over 16 hours), and motor coach tours through the Highlands became popular. In 1930, the horsedrawn coach service between Edzell and Lochlee, Angus, said to have been the last in Scotland, was withdrawn.

Coastal shipping was affected too: in 1929 for instance MacBrayne replaced the Crinan Canal steamer by a bus, and soon afterwards, the Crinan-to-Oban steamer as well – a bus went direct from Ardrishaig to Oban. More and more ships and boats were being fitted with internal combustion engines instead of steam. Diesel engines were often used, being generally larger and more robust than petrol engines. (The difference is that in petrol engines the fuel is ignited by an electric spark, but in diesel engines oil fuel is compressed until it gets so hot that it ignites of its own accord.)

Motor cars were becoming popular, as mass production made them less expensive. Narrow and winding roads were ill-suited to motor traffic, but improvements were slow to come, even though

cars had been taxed to pay for them since about 1910. During the 1920s a new road for motor traffic was built between Edinburgh and Glasgow, and in 1933 another was opened between Tyndrum and Glencoe on the route from Glasgow to Fort William. In 1936 the Ministry of Transport in London took charge of the 1,948 miles of 'trunk roads' (the most important main roads) in Scotland.

In 1937 the railways responded to the challenge of private motoring by putting on very fast express trains hauled by streamlined steam locomotives. These brought the journey times for Euston to Glasgow (LMS) down to six and a half hours, and King's Cross to Edinburgh (LNER) down to six.

But by then the aeroplane, too, was challenging older forms of transport. As early as 1919, during a rail strike, the Post Office had used aircraft to carry the mails between London and Glasgow, and in the 1920s travellers in a hurry could charter aircraft in Scotland. The first Scottish scheduled air services started in 1933, from Glasgow to Campbeltown and Islay, and from Inverness to Kirkwall. The Orkney inter-island service started the following year. By 1939 airline companies, such as Scottish Airlines Ltd and Railway Air Services Ltd which was owned by the railway companies, were serving also Shetland and the Western Isles, Edinburgh and Aberdeen and (from Scotland) Birmingham and London. Then came the Second World War, and all transport had to concentrate again on wartime needs.

Motor bus crosses the Forth & Clyde Canal's lifting bridge at Kirkintilloch.

Nationalization, and

Parked cars throng St Enoch Square, Glasgow, in the 1950s. On the right is the railway station, since closed, also air terminal and airport coach.

During 1948-9 almost all public transport in Britain was nationalized: that is to say it was taken over by the government from the companies which had owned it, and whose shareholders were paid compensation. The British Transport Commission was formed by the government to run railways, canals, road haulage for freight, buses (outside large cities which ran their own), and the Clyde steamers which had belonged to railway companies. Railways throughout Britain were called British Railways and divided into regions: railways in Scotland, from both LMS and LNER, were incorporated into a single Scottish region.

So vast an undertaking proved inefficient. During the 1960s it was split up: British Railways Board ('British Rail' for short) forming one undertaking, British Waterways Board (canals) another, Scottish Transport Group (Scottish buses, and Clyde and West Coast steamers) a third, and so on. Road haulage has mostly been de-nationalized.

It was during the years following the Second World War that the greatest use was made of bus services. Then, as the country recovered from the war, people became steadily more prosperous. Many bought cars for the first time, and ceased to use buses and trains regularly. Motor cars became the everyday means of transport. Similarly, motor lorries became the everyday means of transport for freight. More and more of both poured on to the roads. City streets became clogged by traffic jams. Where there were still trams, it seemed that they obstructed other traffic too much, and they were replaced by buses. Glasgow's trams were the last to go, in 1962. Parked cars obstructed traffic too – so parking meters were installed to reduce their numbers, and multi-storey car parks were built.

Control of trunk roads had reverted to Scotland in 1956 when responsibility for them was transferred from the Ministry of Transport to the Scottish Office in Edinburgh. Improvements to fit them for fast dense traffic were much needed: widenings, straightenings, strong bridges and bypasses to avoid towns and

Motoring for the Millions
1945 – 1982

In the early 1950s, new electric tramcars were still being built for Glasgow.

villages. The work has been done gradually and steadily and still continues.

The A74 Glasgow-Carlisle road was to be made into a dual carriageway and a bypass was needed to avoid Hamilton and Larkhall. About 1960 it was decided to build this as a motorway: an entirely new road, for motor traffic only, dual carriageway, and without crossroads – crossing all other roads (and railways) by bridges. Such roads had been built in Europe since the 1930s and the first part of the M1 motorway in England had been opened in 1959. The first motorway in Scotland to be completed, however, was a four-mile bypass for the village of Harthill on the A8 Edinburgh-Glasgow road: it was opened in 1964 and now forms part of the M8. The first part of the Hamilton bypass was opened, as the M74, in 1966 and since then motorways have been much extended.

Yet in the same period there were parts of the Highlands into which roads were being built for the first time ever. For example, in 1963 road replaced footpath between Shieldaig and Torridon (Ross & Cromarty), and in 1966 between Lochailort and Kinlochmoidart (Inverness-shire).

More spectacular are the great bridges which have been built to close gaps in the road network, often replacing ferries. The Forth Road Bridge was completed in 1964, the Tay Road Bridge in 1966, the Erskine Bridge across the Clyde in 1971. More recently bridges have been built across Loch Leven at Ballachulish and the Moray Firth at Inverness.

This train took children home to Killin from school in Callander.

Electric trains like this went into service on Glasgow suburban lines in the early 1960s.

Puffers were small steamers which for a century carried cargo through the canals, along the coasts and out to the islands. By the 1970s almost all had gone out of use but this one had been converted to take parties of young people on holiday. Seen here on the Caledonian Canal.

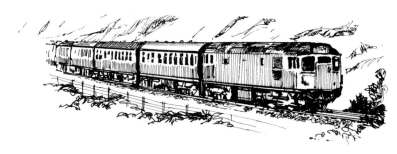

By the 1970s, diesel locomotives had replaced steam.

Air services within Scotland were taken over in 1947 by government-owned British European Airways. During the 1960s air traffic increased rapidly, some of it again carried by independent airlines. Inevitably, increased traffic by road and air meant less traffic by rail and sea. Many more branch lines were closed. So were some main lines, such as Edinburgh to Carlisle via Hawick in 1969: there was no longer enough traffic to support three main lines between Edinburgh and the English border. But much was being done to modernise the railways which survived. Diesel and electric trains are generally faster, cheaper and cleaner to run than steam, so diesel trains and locomotives were introduced widely during the 1950s and early 60s. A fast diesel train service replaced steam trains between Edinburgh and Glasgow in 1957, and in 1967 British Rail ceased to run steam locomotives in Scotland. Glasgow suburban lines were electrified from 1961 onwards, and the main line between Carlisle and Glasgow Central was electrified in 1974, completing electrification from Euston.

Canals and coastal shipping went much the same way as branch line railways. The Forth & Clyde Canal was closed to navigation in 1963, the Union and Monkland Canals had been virtually disused since the 1930s. Much of the Monkland's route was used for the M8 Motorway. British Waterways Board's canals were classified in 1968 as either commercial waterways, for use mainly by barges or ships carrying freight, or cruising waterways for pleasure cruising, or the remainder, to be treated as cheaply as possible, whether they were retained or filled in. The Caledonian and Crinan Canals became commercial waterways and the other Scottish canals became part of 'the remainder'.

Shipping services along the West Coast and the Clyde were steadily withdrawn. There had been an important development in 1954, however, when three new ships went into service to carry not only passengers and cargo but also motor vehicles which drove on and off under their own power – previously they had been loaded and unloaded by crane. Eventually in 1972 the government announced its policy that services to the islands, on the most important routes, should comprise 'roll-on, roll-off' ships to carry road vehicles by the shortest practicable sea crossings.

Discovery of oil beneath the North Sea – the first was brought ashore in 1975 – resulted in a great increase of traffic to north and north-east Scotland, where oil rigs were built and supply bases set up. So airports were enlarged, roads improved – notably the A9 trunk road between Perth and Invergordon – and the second track reinstated where it had been taken out on the Perth-Inverness railway.

Motor vessel *Bute* was one of the first drive-on, drive-off car-carrying ships on the Clyde.

Most small car ferries between points on the mainland have been replaced by bridges, but Corran Ferry across Loch Linnhe is still in use though larger vessels have replaced this one.

Transport Today

There are something like 1,500,000 motor vehicles in Scotland, and over 31,000 miles of public roads. To be precise about the number of vehicles is difficult, because of course they are constantly coming and going across the border, particularly during the summer tourist season, but at the end of 1982 vehicles licensed in Scotland included 1,140,464 cars, 56,588 motor cycles, and 115,969 goods vehicles.

In 1983 there were 147 miles of motorways, mostly on the routes radiating from Edinburgh to Perth, Stirling, and Glasgow and Greenock, and the 348 miles of other dual carriageways. A system of 1,940 miles of trunk roads, including all but fifteen miles of the motorways, extended throughout the mainland. The government, through the Scottish Office, pays (out of peoples' taxes) for building, improving and maintaining trunk roads, but the actual work is organised by the regional councils which replaced county councils in 1975. Regional and island councils are themselves responsible for all other public roads which include another 4,700 miles of important main roads. Roll-on, roll-off ships and ferries link the roads of the mainland with those of the principal islands.

Despite the emphasis on cars and roads there are public transport services throughout Scotland, by bus, coach, train, ship, boat and 'plane, for those who do not wish to use a car or cannot do so – in 1981 it was estimated that nearly half the households in Scotland did not have a car. Many of these services are subsidised: the government or the regions contribute money to the operators who keep fares down. Most also take parcels or freight as well as passengers.

Until recently buses in Glasgow have been run by Strathclyde Passenger Transport Executive, and in Edinburgh, Aberdeen and Dundee by Lothian, Grampian and Tayside Regions respectively, but new laws mean that buses in these cities may now be run by companies. Most buses elsewhere are operated by Scottish Bus Group, which runs them under fleet names such as Eastern Scottish, Highland, and so on, and is itself part of Scottish Transport Group. There are also many small operators who operate a few buses over a few routes. But bus routes now no longer have to be licensed by the government, so there will probably be more

Scottish Bus Group: Highland bus beside Loch Ness.

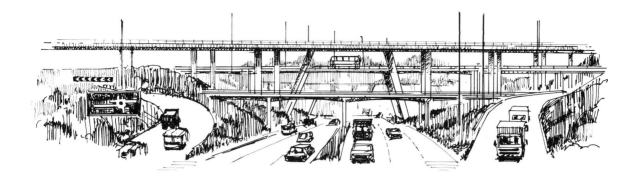

independent operators. Postbuses — minibuses operated by the Post Office — carry passengers as well as mails over rural routes where a mail van would be running anyway and there is no public transport. There are about 135 Postbus services throughout rural Scotland from Galloway to Shetland.

Long-distance motor coach services are operated by Scottish Bus Group between Scotland and places in England (for example, Glasgow to London, fastest time 7 hours 10 minutes via the M6 motorway) and over many routes within Scotland. Licensing for long-distance coach services was abolished in 1980 and several new independent operators have established routes such as Stage Coach's service from Inverness and Perth to Birmingham and London.

There are three main types of passenger train services in Scotland now, operated by British Rail's Scottish Region under the name Scotrail. Inter-city services link the main cities with each other and with England (diesel high speed trains go from King's Cross to Edinburgh in 4 hours 35 minutes, and electric trains from Euston to Glasgow in 5 hours 10 minutes). Glasgow has its network of suburban services, and in remote parts of the country, train services have been retained (to Mallaig, Kyle of Lochalsh and Wick, for example) because to close them would cause too much hardship - rail is more reliable than road in a severe winter.

Train and bus services connect with the main shipping services to the islands, and from Stranraer to Larne in Northern Ireland. There are also still a great many services by small ferries and motor boats. Some of these cross firths and sea lochs, others connect islands with the mainland or each other. Some operate excursions.

Boats still provide essential transport between Scottish islands. These connect North Uist with Berneray.

The beach serves as the airport on the Island of Barra, Western Isles.

Packet boat *Victoria* runs pleasure cruises on the Union Canal at Linlithgow.

The Highlands & Islands Development Board timetable lists 120 ship and boat services in its area alone. At the other extreme, the oil boom has meant that of all the ports in Britain, Shetland now has the greatest weight of traffic passing through: oil brought ashore at Sullom Voe by pipeline from North Sea oilfields is dispatched by tanker.

The busiest airport in Scotland is Glasgow, where about two and a half million passengers start or finish their journeys each year. The least busy is probably Tiree with five thousand. Other important airports are Aberdeen and Edinburgh, mostly used for traffic within Britain, and Prestwick for international traffic. Airlines are British Airways (successors to British European Airways) and independents such as Loganair. Services are mostly between Scottish airports and English ones (the super shuttle between London and Edinburgh or Glasgow takes 1 hour 10 minutes in the air, though the journey from city centre to city centre takes longer), and from mainland airports to and from the islands of the Hebrides, Orkney and Shetland.

The Caledonian and Crinan Canals, though commercial waterways, are now much used by motor cruisers and yachts. After the Forth & Clyde and Union Canals were closed, parts of them were filled in, and bridges which obstructed road traffic were replaced by embankments with small culverts for the water. But between obstructions these canals remain in existence, and pleasure boats have reappeared. People now realise how interesting and enjoyable canals can be – so what is left of them, including many historic features such as bridges and aqueducts, will probably be kept, and some obstructions to boats removed. Indeed in Coatbridge part of the Monkland Canal which had been filled in has now been excavated again and filled with water.

These canals are among the best and most extensive reminders of transport's past. But there are many others. Great viaducts still span valleys although the railways they carried have been dismantled, while elsewhere modern trains still use well-kept Victorian stations. Roadside toll houses and coaching inns survive from the turnpike era, cars drive through the Highlands over roads and bridges designed by Telford, walkers follow routes which once saw droves of cattle.

Even now there are many passes in the Highlands through which roads have never been built, where there are only footpaths. Take a walk along one of them on a May day when an unexpected gale tears spray from waterfalls high on the hillsides to join the clouds drifting around the crags, and if your parents can be persuaded to take you – why, then, within a couple of hundred yards you are travelling as our forefathers did everywhere until 300 years ago. Cars, trains, carriage roads and the rest might never have been invented! As the hailstones fly in your face while you descend from the pass, it is easy to suppose you are on a journey of three weeks or more. With luck you will find cosy shelter for the night in a black house with stone walls and heather thatch and a cauldron bubbling over the open fire in the centre of the floor . . . And then of course what you do find is your own family car waiting to take you home again to the present day. Wherever we go in Scotland, we are constantly reminded of how our forefathers travelled.

Many people regretted the disappearance of steam locomotives and steamships from everyday use, and got together to preserve some in working order. The *West Highlander* train is hauled by a preserved steam locomotive between Fort William and Mallaig; paddle steamer *Waverley* is seen here cruising down the Clyde with Erskine Bridge in the background.

Places to Visit

Aberdeen Maritime Museum, Provost Ross's House, Shiprow, Aberdeen AB1 2BY. Displays relating to local ships and shipping. Tel: 0224 585788.

Barony Chambers Museum, The Cross, Cowgate, Kirkintilloch G66 1PW. (Strathkelvin District Council) Canal and railway exhibits. Tel: 041-775 1185.

Bo'ness & Kinneil Railway, Bo'ness Station, Union Street, Bo'ness EH51 0AD. (Scottish Railway Preservation Society) Passenger-carrying steam railway. Tel: 0506 822298.

Brechin Railway Preservation Society, The Station, 2 Park Road, Brechin, Angus. Locomotives and coaches.

Doune Motor Museum, Doune, Perthshire FK16 6HD. Motor cars. Tel: 0786 841 203.

Fort William — Mallaig steam excursions, Passenger trains hauled over BR line by preserved steam locomotives. Enquiries to British Rail, Fort William Station, Inverness-shire.

Glasgow Museum of Transport. Closed 1987 for transfer to Kelvin Hall, Glasgow. Reopening Spring 1988. The most extensive transport collection in Scotland, including trams, buses, bicycles, motor cycles, coaches and other horsedrawn vehicles, steam road vehicles, motor cars, locomotives and other railway exhibits and ship models. Tel: 041-423 8000 (until September 1987, subsequently 041-357 3929).

Glenesk Folk Museum, The Retreat, Glenesk, Angus. Display relating to horsedrawn coaches between Edzell and Lochlee.

Grampian Transport Museum, Alford, Aberdeenshire AB3 8AD. Motor vehicles, steam road vehicles. Railway exhibits in restored station. Tel: 0336 2292.

Grangemouth Museum, Victoria Library, Bo'ness Road, Grangemouth. Exhibits relating to canals and the *Charlotte Dundas*.

Hamilton District Museum, 129 Muir Street, Hamilton ML3 6BJ. Horsedrawn vehicles and motor cars in a former coaching inn. Tel: 0698 283981.

Kirkcaldy District Museums, War Memorial Gardens, Kirkcaldy, Fife KY1 1YG. (Kirkcaldy District Council) Display with sections on local road, rail and water (ferry) transport. Horsedrawn vehicles: collection to be moved, enquire for location. Tel: 0592 260732.

Linlithgow Union Canal Society Museum, Manse Road Basin, Linlithgow, West Lothian. Canal exhibits in former canal stables beside the Union Canal. Passenger cruises. Tel: 0506 843 654.

Lochty Railway, Lochty Farm, Crail, Fife. Passenger-carrying steam railway. Enquiries to Lochty Railway, Balbuthie, Leven, Fife. Tel: 0592 264587.

McLean Museum & Art Gallery, 9 Union Street, Greenock PA16 8JH. Shipping exhibits. Tel: 0475 23741.

Melrose Motor Museum, Annay Road, Melrose. See Myreton Motor Museum below.

Mull & West Highland Railway, Steam and diesel passenger-carrying miniature railway, Craignure — Torosay Castle, Isle of Mull. Enquiries to Mull & West Highland Railway, The Smiddy House, Aros, Isle of Mull, Argyll PA72 6JB.

MV *Ferry Queen*, Former Clyde ferry runs passenger cruises on the Forth & Clyde Canal from Glasgow Road Bridge, Kirkintilloch. Forth & Clyde Canal Society, c/o T Lawton, 9 Southesk Gardens, Bishopbriggs.

Myreton Motor Museum, Aberlady, East Lothian. Extensive collection of motor cars, motor cycles, old road signs etc. Part of collection forms Melrose Motor Museum. Tel: 087 57 288.

National Museums of Scotland. Tel: 031-225 7534:

  Royal Museum of Scotland, Queen Street, Edinburgh (formerly National Museum of Antiquities of Scotland). Relics of Roman Transport.

  Royal Museum of Scotland, Chambers Street, Edinburgh EH1 1JF (formerly Royal Scottish Museum). Full-size and model exhibits relating to railways (including actual 1814 locomotive *Wylam Dilly*), road vehicles and ships.

  Museum of Flight, East Fortune Airfield, North Berwick, East Lothian EH39 5LF. Aircraft, including some which operated Scottish routes. Tel: 062088 308.

National Tramway Museum, Crich, Matlock, Derbyshire. Glasgow electric tramcars carry passengers on demonstration tramway.

Paisley Museum & Art Gallery, High Street, Paisley PA1 2BA. Display relating to Paisley Canal. Tel: 041-889 3151.

Prestongrange Mining Museum, Morrison's Haven, Prestonpans, East Lothian. Locomotives and other railway exhibits.

PS *Waverley* (Paddle Steamer Preservation Society), Former Clyde paddle steamer runs cruises on the Clyde, West Coast and elsewhere. Enquiries to Waverley Excursions Ltd, Waverley Terminal, Anderston Quay, Glasgow G3 8HA. Tel: 041-221 8152.

Scottish Maritime Museum, Laird Forge, Gottries Road, Irvine KA12 8QE. New and fast developing museum. Historic ships (you can go on board some of them) and many other exhibits relating to ships and shipbuilding.

Scottish Railway Preservation Society, Springfield Yard, Wallace Street, Falkirk FK2 7DR. Locomotives, carriages and wagons. Tel: 0324 20790.

Shetland Museum, Lower Hillhead, Lerwick, Shetland ZE1 0EL. Ship models and other material relating to steamers which served the islands. Tel: 0595 5057.

SS *Sir Walter Scott*, Steamship built 1900 carries passengers on Loch Katrine, Trossachs Pier to Stronachlachar. Enquiries to Water Department, Strathclyde Regional Council, 419 Balmore Road, Glasgow G22 6NU.

Steam Launch *The Lady Rowena*, Passenger cruises on Loch Awe, Argyll, from Loch Awe station pier. Enquiries to Dalriada Steam Packet Co. Ltd., 9 Weymouth Drive, Glasgow G12 0LX. Tel: 041-334 2529.

Strathallan Airfield Collection, Auchterarder, Perthshire PH3 1LA. Aircraft. Tel: 076 46 2545.

Strathspey Railway, The Station, Boat of Garten, Inverness-shire PH24 3BH. Passenger-carrying steam railway, Aviemore — Boat of Garten. Tel: 047 983 692.

Summerlee Heritage Park, West Canal Street, Coatbridge ML5 1QB. Museum of Scottish heavy industry being developed alongside restored section of Monkland Canal. Plans include working electric tramway. Tel: 0236 34930.

Acknowledgements

I am particularly grateful for the assistance provided by Mrs Carol John, librarian of the Scottish Office, and John Clayson, assistant keeper of Glasgow Museum of Transport, during preparation of this book. The staffs of the Scottish Library, Edinburgh, the National Library of Scotland, and Barony Chambers Museum, Kirkintilloch, were also most helpful.

Certain of the illustrations are based on material provided by Glasgow Museum of Transport, PR Consultants (Scotland) on behalf of British Airways, Scottish Transport Group, Strathkelvin District Libraries and Museums, Myreton Motor Museum and Hamilton District Museum, to all of whom I am most grateful.